The Inter-Go Conference: for Building a More Democratic and Effective European Union

Nicholas Hopkinson

August 1996

Wilton Park Paper 122

Report based on Wilton Park Conference 469: 20–24 May 1996 on 'The 1996 IGC: Building A More Effective and Democratic European Union', and Wilton Park Conference 453: 13–17 November 1995 on 'Eurofederalism? Prospects For the 1996 Inter-Governmental Conference'.

London: The Stationery Office

ISBN 0 11 701913 5
ISSN 0953 8542

Published by The Stationery Office and available from:

The Publications Centre
(mail, telephone and fax orders only)
PO Box 276, London SW8 5DT
General enquiriezs 0171 873 0011
Telephone orders 0171 873 9090
Fax orders 0171 873 8200

The Stationery Office Bookshops
49 High Holborn, London WC1V 6HB
(counter service and fax orders only)
Fax 0171 831 1326
68-69 Bull Street, Birmingham B4 6AD
0121 236 9696 Fax 0121 236 9699
33 Wine Street, Bristol BS1 2BQ
0117 926 4306 Fax 0117 929 4515
9-21 Princess Street, Manchester M60 8AS
0161 834 7201 Fax 0161 833 0634
16 Arthur Street, Belfast BT1 4GD
01232 238451 Fax 01232 235401
The Stationery Office Oriel Bookshop
The Friary, Cardiff CF1 4AA
01222 395548 Fax 01222 384347
71 Lothian Road, Edinburgh EH3 9AZ
(counter service only)

Customers in Scotland may
mail, telephone or fax their orders to:
Scottish Publications Sales
South Gyle Crescent, Edinburgh EH12 9EB
0131 479 3141 Fax 0131 479 3142

Accredited Agents
(see Yellow Pages)

and through good booksellers

Contents

1   Introduction

The Treaty on European Union (TEU) signed at Maastricht launched a new phase of greater European co-operation. The TEU has had less than three years to prove itself, a time span which some believe is too short to permit properly founded judgements to be passed. Nevertheless, Article N, Paragraph 2 of the TEU called for the revision of various provisions of the TEU in 1996 in order to assess progress in fulfilling the TEU's objectives. Thus in March 1996, the Inter-Governmental Conference (IGC) commenced in Turin to reflect on and move forward the Maastricht process.

The focus of the IGC has shifted from seeking to finish business left over from Maastricht towards preparing Europe for the future. The European Union (EU) must find answers to contemporary challenges, whilst at the same time making them understandable and acceptable to EU citizens. Accepting this argument, the European Council in Madrid stated that efforts must be made to increase citizen-friendliness and transparency of EU procedures and institutions, and the Turin meeting set this as an IGC objective. The IGC also aims to create a more efficient EU, and to improve the EU's ability to negotiate and act in external matters. The composition of the Commission, the Presidency of the Council, the extension of Qualified Majority Voting (QMV) and the reweighting of votes in the Council are sensitive issues on which a convergence of views will be difficult to achieve. Member States differ over the degree to which sovereignty should be transfered and in which areas. For example, many believe there should be more QMV in the first pillar (except tax), and that there should be scope for some communitisation in the second (Common Foreign and Security Policy) and especially third (Justice and Home Affairs) pillars.

The IGC must be seen in the context of other major issues. One of the most important driving forces behind the IGC is enlargement. Without reform of EU institutional structures and procedures, enlargement would weaken the EU's political cohesion. Jacques Delors said "in enlarging the EU, we need to avoid getting bogged down in an entity without cohesion, without an institutional spine, without the ability to decide and act". Economic and Monetary Union (EMU), which will not be discussed at the IGC, is regarded by many as more important than institutional *and* other issues that will be discussed at the IGC. Also important is the EU's economic competitiveness, which a few Member States have asked to be discussed at the IGC. This paper will therefore examine issues before the IGC as well as the parallel issues of EMU and economic competitiveness that will have to be addressed as the EU enters the twenty-first century.

2 What Kind of Europe?

There are several terms used to describe the pattern and speed of EU integration including a multispeed, variable geometry and an à la carte Europe. Germany and the Benelux countries favour greater integration in most areas and a core of Member States to take forward the integration process. However, some Member States are unwilling to deepen integration in order to secure a further enlargement. The government of the United Kingdom (UK) has advocated flexibility as a solution to the diverse views held by Member States. Some British Ministers have even suggested that some powers be repatriated, but this raises the issue of what the EU's core functions are. The French position appears to envisage some flexibility in the second and third pillars but no flexibility in the first pillar.

At the heart of the IGC debate is the issue of whether a more flexible EU would weaken its cohesiveness. A clause on flexibility is being debated as part of a new draft treaty. It is argued that a more flexible EU containing a critical mass of more integrated countries encourages the general purpose of EU integration.

However, some argue that a general clause in a new Treaty allowing a group of countries to develop enhanced co-operation without any specific conditions and prerequisites is incompatible with the cohesiveness of the EU. Flexibility can be regarded as an easy way around controversial substantive issues. There is likely to be little scope for flexibility in the first pillar as EU legislation must be uniform throughout the EU. In the second pillar, the Franco-German concept of 'constructive abstention' may offer a way forward, but retention of a national veto will probably be unavoidable if an issue is judged to be one key to the national interest. Therefore, it appears that the most scope for flexibility lies in the third pillar.

Recognising the difference of views among Member States, the IGC Reflection Group agreed on the following criteria for the adoption of a flexible framework: the single institutional framework and the 'acquis communautaire' have to be respected (the EU and EU institutions cannot be used to apply prefered national policies or distort EU activity); recourse to flexibility should be considered on a case-by-case basis when all other solutions have been ruled out (last resort); derogations should not be allowed in the Community pillar if they jeopardise the internal market, however the second and third pillars may offer the possibility of a greater degree of flexibility; differences in the degree of integration should, in principle, be temporary and agreed by all; no one who so desires and fulfils the necessary conditions can be excluded from full participation in a given action or common policy; and provision should be made for *ad hoc* measures to assist those who want to take part in a given action or policy but are temporarily unable to do so.

It is important that the IGC balances the conflicting goals of efficiency and legitimacy. The concept of subsidiarity, anchored in Article 3b of the TEU, is an important structural principle which maintains not only diversity in Europe but also the proper functioning of different EU institutions. Subsidiarity enhances legitimacy as well as acceptance. Therefore a new treaty must make the concept of subsidiarity more operational.

Enlargement: the Impetus for Reforming the EU

The impending enlargement of the EU is the major force driving the EU to reform and deepen integration. EU enlargement therefore depends on the reform of EU institutions, procedures and policies as well as candidates' own efforts to meet the EU's entry requirements.

The EU has become a strong pole of attraction to its neighbours for political, economic and security reasons. The EU is not an exclusive, inward-looking club: Article O of the TEU provides that any European state may apply to become a member. The Copenhagen European Council in June 1993 committed the EU to admitting all Central and East European Countries (CEECs) as soon as they are able to satisfy economic and political conditions, namely political stability, democratic institutions, the rule of law, and respect for human rights and ethnic minorities. Candidates must have a market economy and a capacity to cope with competitive market forces. Eventually they must qualify for EMU. These prerequisites are coupled with the proviso that the EU has the capacity to absorb new members, and to maintain the momentum of European integration. The European Parliament (EP) reiterated the latter point by stating: "a possible over-hasty accession by the CEECs on purely political grounds would undermine the internal market itself and would result in the EU functioning less efficiently".[1]

Enlargement is not a cost-free process: the EU will have to ensure that resources are sufficient to finance common policies. While the enlargement to Malta and Cyprus will have only a minimal impact on the EU budget, an eastern enlargement will be more costly given the large number of applicant countries with different political, economic and social structures. In order to prepare for the smooth integration of CEECs, a wide-ranging pre-accession strategy has been established, through Association Agreements, the structured dialogue, initiated at the Essen 1994 European Council, and the PHARE programme of financial assistance.

---

[1] European Parliament Resolution on Enlargement (A4-0101/17.4.96)

The issues relating to the accession of Malta and Cyprus differ from those relating to the accession of the CEECs. Cyprus represents potential legal, practical and political problems if it joins before a settlement of the division of the island. But economically there is little difficulty. Malta and Cyprus are small in terms of population and size and their economic situation is relatively robust. Cyprus' GDP per capita is higher than that of Spain, Portugal and Greece. Inflation is only three per cent and unemployment is estimated to be 2.6 per cent. The current deficit is 2.7 per cent and accumulated debt is 55 per cent, both well below the Maastricht EMU convergence criteria. The General Affairs Council of March 1995, reconfirmed at Cannes and Madrid Councils, agreed that negotiations with Cyprus and Malta will start six months after the conclusion of the IGC. In order assuage CEEC applicants, the Madrid Council "expressed the hope that the preliminary stage of negotiations with CEECs will coincide with the start of negotiations with Cyprus and Malta". No linkage was introduced between the applications of Malta and Cyprus and those of CEECs though nothing precludes negotiations with all applicants starting at the same time.

Existing and potential candidates need considerable pre-accession assistance in the form of modernisation programmes, technical assistance and access to the EU's market, in order to narrow the differences that exist between the EU and CEEC levels of development. One important indicator of this gap is the agricultural sector's share of overall output and the workforce: agriculture accounts for 2.5 per cent of the EU's GDP compared with 7.8 per cent of CEEC combined GDP; and 5.7 per cent of the EU work force is employed in agriculture compared with 26.7 per cent of the CEEC workforce.

EU Member States with heavily subsidised agricultural sectors and poor regions are worried about how the imperative for enlargement is placing pressure on the EU to reform the Common Agricultural Policy (CAP) and the structural funds. Member States with heavily subsidised agricultural sectors are essentially playing for time: they argue that the EU still has to implement the Blair House Accord, Uruguay Round measures and the 1992

McSharry reform of the CAP. Not surprisingly, many Member States ensured that the CAP and structural funds would not be discussed at the IGC, but would be discussed separately in 1999.

Estimates of the cost of all 10 CEECs joining the CAP vary considerably. Professor Richard Baldwin estimates that the entry of the Visegrad Four would require an additional cost to the EU budget of ECU 47 billion. The UK's Ministry of Agriculture forecasts ECU 25 billion would be required. A study by the Commission submitted to the Madrid Council in December 1995 forecasts a more conservative figure of about nine billion ECU in 2000, rising to ECU 12 billion in 2010 assuming that 1995 CAP expenditure remains unchanged.

Although the EU is the most important financial contributor to the CEECs, this sum is low compared to what the EU gives to the four EU cohesion countries: for example, Ireland received $260 per head and Portugal $170 per head compared to only $30 per head for citizens of six CEECs.

The amount earmarked for economic and social cohesion is scheduled to rise from ECU 26.3 billion in 1995, or 35 per cent of the EU budget, to ECU 33 billion in 1999. To maintain the current cohesion effort and apply an equivalent effort to the CEECs could easily double this figure. In order to cope with this increase, two basic options have been advanced: increase the EU budget to accommodate new Member States, or maintain the same level of expenditure, thus redirecting part of the funds, currently used for cohesion of existing Member States, to finance an eastward enlargement. Thus, Member States whose income lags behind the EU average would have to meet a disproportionately large part of the cost of enlargement, thereby impeding the cohesion process. However, Commissioner Woulf-Mathies stated "beginning enlargement without guaranteeing the EU's least prosperous countries that the cohesion policy will be maintained and even reinforced, would be socially and politically unthinkable". In order to avoid compromising EU solidarity, either by failing to meet the needs of existing members or avoiding the financial implications of future enlargement, a considerable increase in the overall size of the budget appears to be necessary. However, in the end, in 1999 the EU, in part required by the financial constraints of EMU, is likely to agree further reductions in the CAP and structural funds. This, in turn, will reduce the budgetary consequences of enlargement, thus improving the chances of a broader accession.

Transitional measures and arrangements have been used in the past to facilitate the smooth integration of new members. However, in view of the high cost of the new enlargement, transitional measures are also being envisaged as a means to restrict EU spending. The capacity of new members to absorb considerable transfers will have to be taken into consideration. However, any attempt to impose long transitional periods mainly for the purpose of excluding the applicant countries from most of the financial benefits of membership would forfeit the EU's objective of strengthening economic and social cohesion. By the same token, depriving the new members of their voting rights on issues such as, for example, the CAP and structural funds, would create strong resentment amongst the newcomers: it would be equivalent to relegating them to the rank of second class partners. Nevertheless, Poland, the second CEEC to submit its application, has indicated that it would renounce its claim to structural funds and CAP allowances. This suggests that Poland, and perhaps other candidates, may be willing to accept 'partial' EU membership.

Candidates hope that they will not become hostage to a prolonged IGC, and that accession negotiations will commence soon after the conclusion of the IGC. They hope that the IGC will be well managed and that its agenda is neither too broad nor too narrow. Candidates, frustrated with the overly-formal structured dialogue with the EU, would have prefered to have had observer status at the IGC as this would have helped them to become more effective Member States after accession. Furthermore, as future EU Member States, they believe that should have a say in the development of a group that they are likely to join.

A number of arguments are used to downplay the possibility of an early eastern enlargement for many CEECs. For example, it is argued that if CEECs are admitted to the Single Market too soon, then they would be unable to compete and to adopt fully the necessary regulations. However, the EU should not underestimate the capacity of CEECs to adapt, especially as they have adopted stricter market reforms than EU Member States themselves. It is argued that in the pre-membership period, CEECs should concentrate more on regional free trade. Although the Central European Free Trade Area (CEFTA) is a stepping stone to greater Europe-wide economic integration, CEFTA's impact will be limited because all CEEC economies are essentially competitors, offering the same products and exports. After three years, optimum regional trade will have been attained. It is also argued that only a few CEECs will actually join the EU in the next five years. The Czech Republic, one of the most likely new members, is well qualified for early membership because it has a high economic growth rate, low unemployment, no poor regions, and a small agricultural sector. However, arguments against an early accession tend to look at the costs of enlargement rather its benefits to existing Member States. Overall, CEECs can only contribute to the EU's competitiveness and to geo-political stability in Europe.

3 Improving Transparency, Efficiency and Accountability of the EU

Improving transparency is an important element in the further democratisation of the EU. Furthermore, it may be a precondition for the successful ratification of any treaty resulting from the IGC. Transparency is important as a means of demystifying the workings of the EU and to bridge the gap between policy makers and public opinion. Transparency also facilitates democratic control by parliaments and thus enhances the accountability of EU institutions. Contrary to the popular view, transparency can also improve the efficiency of the EU.

A distinction should be made between the factual and formal situation regarding transparency. Most meetings and papers remain confidential. In the EU's first thirty years, not much thought was given to rules for transparency because the situation was not perceived to be a problem. However, this is no longer the case because many Member States with a tradition of open government have joined the EU. With the increasing political interest in transparency, the Community itself has changed. Thus in reality, EU decision- making is now more open than that of most national administrations. The 15 permanent representatives to the EU and EU institutions brief journalists regularly. Journalists have a better chance of obtaining 'off the record' information or comments in Brussels than in Member State capitals. Therefore, EU institutions are open to those who know where to look for information.

The Community initially dealt mainly with technical questions that only concerned a few sectors of society. Most of those questions traditionally fell within the competence of national executives, rather than parliaments. Over the years, the scope of Community action was extended in response to the growth of cross-border flows of goods, services, money, people and ideas. Increased interdependence required Community-wide actions and solutions. This was particularly the case with the Internal Market Programme which substantially increased the amount of Community legislation. For these reasons Community issues gradually became part of mainstream domestic politics. 'Europe' is no longer just foreign policy. The need for greater democratisation, including transparency, could not be ignored.

During the TEU negotiations, the need to open up the work of EU institutions was not fully understood by decision-makers. Decisions were largely taken behind closed doors. Although the issue of transparency was raised during the Maastricht negotiations, notably by the Danish Government, it never became a central theme. There was merely a declaration in the TEU obliging the Commission to submit a report on measures designed to improve public access to information held by EU institutions.

During the ratification of the TEU, it became clear that public support for the treaty was limited. The simple granting of citizen rights in the TEU did not in itself create a 'citizens' Europe'. The Danish 'no' to the TEU on 2 June 1992, the narrow French 'yes' shortly thereafter, and the heated discussions on the TEU in other Member States clearly showed the need to bring the EU closer to its citizens. One of the most important means to do this is transparency.

The last four years have seen cautious but successive steps towards democratisation and greater transparency. The Birmingham and Edinburgh European Councils responded immediately to the public disquiet expressed during the TEU ratification process. In October 1992, Heads of State and government adopted the Birmingham Declaration which had transparency and subsidiarity as its central themes.

The December 1992 Edinburgh Summit decided there should be improved: access to information (the Commission was asked to speed up its work); access to the work of the Council; information on the role of the Council and its decisions, and easier access to Community legislation. With these decisions now implemented, the EU is considerably more open than before. On the whole the new rules function fairly well and do represent an important step forward. For example, in the field of access to information held by the institutions, the Council and the Commission adopted a Code of Conduct in November 1993. This Code of Conduct was subsequently transformed into legally binding acts by the two institutions. Citizens of the EU thus obtained a statutory right to access to documents. A refusal to meet an application for access could henceforth be brought before the Court, thus bringing EU practice in line with that in a number of Member States.

The rules on access to documents did, however, also provide for a number of exceptions. Some of these were fairly straightforward, for example: protection of the right to privacy of individuals or protection of business secrets. Such exceptions are common to all access to information rules where they exist at the national level. But one exception, wanted by a majority in the Council, was much more dubious. It allowed each institution to protect its "interest in the confidentiality of its proceedings". It is this exception, and in particular the way it has been administered by the Council, that has been the main source of criticism. It was also under this exception that John Carvel of *The Guardian* was denied access to a number of documents of the Council in early 1994. John Carvel took the Council to court. The refusal was annulled in October 1995 by the European Court of First Instance which ruled that the Council had not properly weighed the interest in access of the applicant against the interest in secrecy of the Council.

Access to the work of the Council is one of the most difficult, but also one of the basic aspects of transparency. The Council is increasingly legislating in areas where national Parliaments, with their long standing traditions for open discussion and decision making, were acting. However, the legislative process at both the European and national levels does require some degree of confidentiality to be effective. In all national parliaments, the beginning of the legislative procedure, the first reading of a bill, the final discussion and the vote take place in public. But in most national Parliaments the Committee stage in between allow for confidential work. However, at the EU level, there is no distinction between the various stages. Accordingly, greater transparency at the beginning and at the end of the legislative procedure has been proposed.

At the Edinburgh Summit, the Heads of State and Government decided that there should be public debates in the Council. The rules governing such public debates were inserted in the Council's rules of Procedure in December 1993. They provide for two obligatory debates during each Presidency on the work programme in the General Affairs Council and the Ecofin Council. These types of public debate, presenting an overview of the work of the Council, have been useful. Furthermore, the new rules allow the Council to decide, by unanimity and on a case-by-case basis, to have additional open debates, in particular concerning important issues and important new legislative proposals. Unfortunately, this did not lead to satisfactory results.

First of all, the number of public debates declined from nine during the Danish Presidency in the first half of 1993 to just the two obligatory debates during the German Presidency in the autumn of 1994. Secondly, very few of those debates were about important legislative proposals. The intention, to make the beginning of the legislative proccess more open, had not been fulfilled.

For this reason, a Danish initiative on openness in the legislative work of the Council was proposed in March 1995 which, *inter alia*, called for the rule of unanimity for additional public debates to be changed to a simple majority. Although this proposal was rejected, it was agreed that there should be a declaration from the Council saying that there should be more public debate, and that the Presidency should make proposals to this effect at the beginning of each Presidency. As a result, the Spanish Presidency proposed a list with 10 public debates, which was accepted by the Council. Neverthelesss, more transparency at the start of the legislative process needs further improvement.

The Edinburgh decision made public the results of formal votes in the Council. Previously it had been a secret whether a country had voted for or against a particular piece of legislation. The implementation of this decision took the form of a new rule inserted in the Council Rules of Procedure in December 1993 which requires votes to be made public when the Council is acting as legislator, unless the Council decides otherwise. When the voting result is made public, explanations of the vote are also made public at the request of the Council Member concerned. Denmark obtained a declaration that the Council would not intend to use the exception clause in the future. Thus, it would be difficult to keep a vote secret. In the event of a leak, the attempted secrecy would most probably attract considerable press attention. This new rule is functioning quite well. In 1994, for example, voting results were published on 261 occasions. However, the publication of votes did not provide sufficient transparency with regard to the final phase of the legislative procedure.

As a minimum, publication of minutes of the Council and declarations of such minutes should be published. The declarations, especially those coming from the Commission and those agreed by the whole Council, often contain important elements of interpretation of the legislative text. Although the result of a March 1995 Danish proposal to make public all minutes and declarations concerning legislation was disappointing, the resulting Code of Conduct was another step in the right direction.

The 2 October 1995 Code of Conduct, an informal agreement rather than a legal text, contains three main elements:

firstly, the use of declarations shall be used with more restraint in the future. A report by the Council legal service has shown that, in the past, an excessive number of declarations have been annexed to some legislative acts. From now on alternatives must be sought. Some declarations could be inserted in the legislative text itself. Others could become explanations of votes and made public as such;

secondly, declarations must in all cases be compatible with the text of the legislative act itself. This ought to be self-evident, but in the past there have been examples of declarations contradicting the legislative text;

thirdly, declarations and minutes will henceforth be made public, unless a Member of the Council requests a vote, and this vote shows that there is not a (simple) majority to do so.

The solution obtained is similar to, if not quite as good as, the one concerning voting records. If implemented in good faith, the Code of Conduct will lead to automatic publication of practically all future declarations and minutes. However, journalists regard the Code of Conduct as inadequate because some documents continue to be protected. A possible solution would be to have an independent system of appeal such as the Swedish Ombudsman system.

The traditional informal openness and access for well-funded organisations and specialists who know where to look will not enough to enhance the transparency of the EU. Wide-ranging rules of secrecy will remain a source of public suspicion and scepticism. Jacques Santer, President of the Commission, has joined the call for greater transparency: "the future of the Community can no longer remain the prerogative of a select band of insiders. Europeans are insisting on making their voices heard, in participating in what has become a central feature of their lives . . . Unless we satisfy those demands our venture will fail".

Transparency is indispensable in the efforts to increase accountability and efficiency of EU institutions. National parliaments as well as the EP can control the Council and the Commission only if they are allowed to know what is going on. It is, therefore, not suprising that the EP and national parliaments increasingly are the driving forces towards greater transparency. If decision-making becomes more transparent, the quality of EU legislation will be enhanced because outside actors will be able to point to possible improvements. Governments and institutions directly involved will become even more determined to produce good results. Bad habits, such as the occasional declaration contrary to the legislative text, will disappear. Results from the legislative process will be easier for national parliaments and populations to understand and to be accepted. This, in turn, will facilitate implementation, making EU legislation not just more efficient but also more effective.

However, complete openness cannot be achieved overnight. Not all meetings can be open. Some papers must continue to be confidential. When the Council performs its executive functions, confidentiality will also often be necessary. There may also be a need for closed doors in some phases of the legislative process in order to allow for genuine negotiations to take place. Otherwise real decision-making might move to less formal fora, perhaps without the participation of all Member States.

There should continue to be a focus on the legislative process, in particular the beginning and the end. Improving transparency in the future could focus on:

a compulsory delay or debating period from the time the Commission puts forward a legislative proposal until work begins in the Council and the EP. This would give all interested parties and national parliaments a chance to put forward their views on the proposal. Reactions received by the Commission could be made public;

the first reading in the Council could take the form of a written procedure on the basis of a questionnaire from the Council Secretariat. The answers to the questionnaire and the written basis for continued discussion in the Council could then be made public. Such a procedure would have the added advantage of doing away with time-consuming round tables, which would significantly enhance efficiency;

after a negotiation phase, the Council could hold a public debate leading to the adoption, in public, of a common position. This would contribute to the popular understanding of how the EU's legislative process works;

after co-decision, assent or consultation of the EP, the Council could take the final vote in public. This would eradicate any remaining doubt as to what individuals ministers vote in Council and show more clearly how decisions are made; and

after adoption of the act, there should be unconditional access to voting results, minutes and declarations. Various types of preparatory documents could be made public once the negotiations are over.

Such steps would combine the need for increased transparency and accountability with the need not just to maintain, but also enhance, the efficiency and effectiveness of the legislative process. They would streamline decision-making and lead to better quality of EU legislation. They could be combined with a clearer statement of the right to access to information as a fundamental principle of the EU. These steps would not necessarily involve Treaty changes. In any case, a new treaty should not be overloaded with detailed technical provisions. However, the fundamental principle of right to access to information as well as the principle of greatest possible openness in the EU legislative process should be stated. Detailed provisions could then be worked out in secondary legislation and in the Council rules of procedure. This would also make it possible to adjust the rules in the light of experience.

4   Reform of Decision-Making

One of the main aims of the IGC is to make the EU's institutions and decision-making procedures more efficient to enable enlargement of the EU. If Member States do not reform EU decision-making sufficiently, there will be a point at which an enlarged EU will simply just cease to function. It would damage the credibility of the EU to have a minimalist result from the current IGC and then be required to convene another inter-governmental conference four years later to ensure that the EU is ready for enlargement. As it is widely believed that the results from the IGC will be modest, it appears that another IGC will be necessary around 2000.

EU decision-making will be paralysed if there are more than 15 Member States. As the EU enlarges, it becomes increasingly difficult to reach decisions by unanimity. The existing system in the first pillar, in which a qualified majority requires 62 votes or 71 per cent of the votes, has generally worked quite well. However, there have been crises, the most famous being the French empty chair in 1965 which was overcome by the so-called Luxembourg compromise. Another threat, which arose in the final phase of enlargement negotiations in Spring 1994, was overcome by the Ioannina compromise. The UK's non co-operation policy during the 1996 beef crisis also temporarily disrupted EU decision-making.

In light of these experiences, Member States have suggested a number of possible reforms of voting in the Council including re-weighting the votes of larger Member States; preserving the principle of unanimity for a limited number of well-defined exceptions such as constitutional issues, accession and association of new members, fiscal policy, own resources and fields deemed to be vital to national interests, and even introducing a 'consensus minus one' voting formula.

The Balance in Decision-Making Between Small and Large States

The issue of the balance in decision-making between small and large states arises in the IGC largely because many smaller countries have applied for full membership of the EU. The EU was founded as a community of large and small Member States and therefore voting in the Council is a balance between the principle of one country, one vote and the relative weight of Member States' populations. The result has been an over-representation of smaller Member States. Thus, for example, the three Benelux countries, with 27 million citizens, have 12 votes while Germany, with 80 million citizens, has only 10 votes.

The IGC will be essentially a bargain between the larger Member States. However small Member States will have an important say. The larger Member States appear determined to increase their weighted vote in the Council. Fearing this, most smaller Member States are reluctant to accept any new formulae that would change the present balance in the Council at their expense. It would be difficult for any government to return from the conclusion of the IGC negotiations and say to its electorate that the country now has fewer votes in the Council.

Many larger Member States often maintain that the main culprit for the lack of effectiveness in the existing decision-making process is each Member State's right to veto and the ability of smaller Member States to form coalitions. Many larger Member States believe that it is not democratic that smaller Member States, whose population is 43 per cent of the EU total, have 73 per cent of the votes while the 57 per cent of the EU's population living in the four largest states have only 27 per cent of the votes. The accession of many small new Member States would further increase the chance of standstill in EU decision-making. Not only will there be the possibility of a 'veto' by a small Member State, but the weight of larger Member States' votes in Council decision-making would be further diluted. For example, if the present vote allocation remains the same, eight small Member States in an EU of 25 Member States would be able to block decisions, while five big Member States would be unable to forge a countering majority.

Germany has no problem with the current disequilibrium in weighted voting because it has traditionally favoured a relatively stronger role for smaller Member States. In the IGC, Germany will seek to avoid taking positions which might lead to an unproductive confrontation between large and small Member States. In any case, votes are not cast according to the size of Member States, but according to the national interest in any given policy area. For example, in agriculture, more heavily subsidised producers (France, Germany, Italy, Autria and Finland) are opposed by the more efficient producers (Denmark, the Netherlands and the UK).

Smaller Member States argue that there have been few, if any, cases when a decision was adopted contrary to the interests of large Member States. The continuation of a fair balance in decision-making between large and small Member States depends on whether the system ensures: institutional equality among Member States; respect for national interests; effective decision-making, and effective implementation of EU policies. These four principles, upon which the integration process was originally founded, should be the cornerstone of any institutional adjustment.

Any new voting system needs to preserve the balance of the current system. One possible compromise is the concept of a double majority in which a certain percentage of weighted Council votes a n d the EU's total population must be exceeded. If, for example, a 70 per cent threshhold is stipulated, three large

Member States could block any decision. A possible refinement would be a double simple majority with a lower threshhold, perhaps 60 per cent, which makes it easier to take decisions. Another possible solution would be the inclusion of economic criteria, such as the size of a Member State's economy or the size of its contribution to the EU budget, in the weight of its Council vote. However, given the experience of the 1983 budget crisis, a link between an economic contribution and Council voting could be especially dangerous.

Not surprisingly, smaller Member States oppose adding new criteria because they would weaken their influence. They argue that adding new criteria violates the fundamental principle of equality of Member States in the Council. They argue that including new criteria could endanger the EU because criteria would de facto introduce national criteria in the voting process; establish a bloc of larger Member States within the Council; introduce discrimination in the EU's institutional structure, and create a balance in weighted voting unfavourable to smaller Member States. Instead smaller Member States advocate a new system based on political will, mutual understanding and political dialogue.

Some argue that the debate between small and large Member States is a difference in tone rather than substance. Balance is an issue in all federal systems. If a double majority system were introduced in the Council, then it should also be introduced in the EP. A bicameral structure, as in the United States, would be the result. Although a bicameral system for some may be easier to accept than an increase in the weighted votes of large countries, such a solution is too radical for the IGC. The Council is, and shall remain, the main decision-making body in the EU.

Simplifying Decision-Making Procedures

In order to make EU decision-making more efficient and to avoid paralysis, more areas should be subject to QMV. Section 21.1 of the Brok-Guigou report on the IGC submitted to the 13 March 1996 sitting of the EP stated: "QMV should become the general procedure within the EU, and this should be one of the central objectives of the IGC". There is also broad agreement in the IGC Reflection Group and amongst most Member States that QMV should be extended to new areas. In particular, many Member States support the extension of QMV to certain sectors of the first pillar, especially the internal market, research, technology, health, and specific sections of the second and third pillars. The EP has further argued that everything that is decided by QMV in the Council should be subject to co-decision by the EP.

Under the TEU, the EP received new powers including increased amending and budgetary powers. But further measures are likely to be taken by the IGC. In particular, decision-making procedures could be simplified to three basic mechanisms: the EP could have the right of co-decision (effectively a veto) in all areas decided by QMV in the Council; the EP could continue to give its assent on budgetary and accession matters, and the EP must continue to be consulted on decisions taken by unanimity of the Council. Access to information should be improved and should be released in time for MEPs and national parliamentarians to influence decisions. A further possibility might be for the EP to exercise more democratic control over EU institutions by agreeing appointments to them.

Section 21.6 of the Brok-Guigou report argues for an even greater increase in the EP's powers: "Co-decision should be extended to *all* legislation. Legislation should be dealt with by a qualified majority in the Council. Annexes shall be explicitly considered as coming under co-decision. The co-decision procedure should be simplified, in particular by dropping the phase of intention to reject, and by ending the procedure either when there is agreement between the Council and the EP (even at first reading) or when there is no agreement between the Council and the EP in a conciliation committee. The EP should be required to give its assent to all Article 235 cases, own resources decisions and in all cases of reform of the Treaty and international agreements".

Section 21.7 further recommends that "the distinction between compulsory and non-compulsory expenditure should be removed; the budget should be unified and budgetary procedures should be simplified. The EP should have as much responsibility for compulsory expenditure as it currently has for non-compulsory expenditure. The IGC should undertake a genuine reform of the own resources system, which should be concluded, at the latest, when the financial perspective in the Inter-Institutional Agreement lapses in 1999. In view of the time needed for this reform, the IGC should begin to formulate proposals now, so that the reformed system can take account of the EU's development".

The IGC should also simplify the existing maze of comitology procedures by transferring overall responsibility for implementing measures to the Commission. Type 2 and 3 committees should be abolished. The Council and the EP should be notified of the measures proposed and each should have the option of rejecting Commission proposals and calling for new implementing measures or the initiation of a full legislative procedure.

5   The Respective Roles of National and European Parliaments

It has been argued that, if EU had to join itself, it would not qualify because it is not sufficiently democratic. The TEU makes the 'democratic deficit' even worse because there is no, or at best little, European and national parliamentary scrutiny of the second and third pillars. In order to improve accountability and legitimacy of the EU, the IGC will have to strengthen the involvement of both national parliaments and the EP in EU decision-making.

National parliaments have no direct European responsibilities. Accordingly, some Member States regard increased national parliamentary scrutiny over EU legislation as more important than reform of EU institutions such as the Presidency and the Commission. Indeed Declaration 13 of the TEU calls for the "greater involvement of national parliaments in the activities of the EU". 'Shared responsibility', as suggested by the Danish model, can be developed even within the first pillar. National parliaments can appeal to the Court of Justice; there should be a right of consultation on issues which are subject to the test of subsidiarity; and there should be a right to question Commissioners on EU legislation. However, a more formal role for national parliaments cannot result in the blocking of EU-wide legislation, lest the efficiency and uniformity of EU legislation is impaired.

Contacts between the EP and national Parliaments, their respective committees, and the exchange of information between national parliaments and the EP can be improved. Direct elections to the EP have ironically weakened links between MEPs and national parliamentarians. Before the first direct elections to the EP in 1979, all MEPs were nominated from their national parliaments so contact between the two levels was close. However, now only a few MEPs are also members of their national parliaments. Hence it has become necessary to find means to improve contacts. In addition to informal contacts, formal contacts have been developed at four levels:

national parliaments have enhanced their role in European decision-making through improved cooperation amongst themselves and through trans-European party links. Declaration 14 of the TEU calls on national parliaments to meet as a conference of the parliaments, or 'assises'. The first conference of EU parliaments in Rome in November 1990 brought together more than 300 MEPs and all 20 chambers of the parliaments of the then 12 Member States;

since 1981, the Presidents and Speakers of EU Parliaments have met every two years. There is no precise agenda or formal conclusions from these meetings because some Presidents and Speakers enjoy a degree of political autonomy while others are unable to make political statements on behalf of their chambers;

since 1989, there have been bi-annual meetings of national parliamentary committees dealing with European Affairs (COSAC). These meetings review cooperative structures and issues, such as the implementation of EU law, in a more detailed way than the Presidents. Building on the COSAC model, a 'grand committee' of EU parliaments has been suggested as a means to improve scrutiny of EU legislation;

the membership of European Affairs committees in some parliaments, namely in Belgium, Greece and Germany, have been structured to include representatives from the EP. Similarly, the EP has been eager to develop contacts with national parliamentarians early in the legislative process. EP committees have invited national parliamentarians to attend EP committee meetings to discuss topics of common interest.[2]

6 The Second and Third Pillars

The second and third pillars are the subject of considerable debate in the IGC.

Common Foreign and Security Policy

The dissolution of the Soviet Union and the end of Communism in CEECs have radically changed the political and security environment in Europe. The resulting security vacuum is not yet filled and the situation is still dangerous. For example, the Ukraine continues to be characterised by internal problems and external threats. The final outcome of the disintegration of the former Soviet Union is still uncertain. Europe cannot rely on the US' future commitment to European security forever.

The TEU's Common Foreign and Security Policy (CFSP) provisions generated high expectations, but the CFSP is widely judged to have been ineffective, in spite of some successes in enlarging and concluding associate memberships. Diplomacy and defence

---

[2] *The EP and National Parliaments*, UK Office of the European Parliament and EP Division for Relations with Parliaments of the Member States (July, 1995).

continue to dominated by the pursuit of national interests. The failure of EU policy in the Former Yugoslavia, and the subsequent success of NATO's intervention, should teach the EU to take the CFSP more seriously. As pointed out in the Council's report to the IGC Reflection Group, the TEU "cannot alone provide solutions to problems but only the means to facilitate them. The political will to act is a determining factor".

The IGC therefore provides an opportunity for Member States to take decisive steps towards a credible and effective CFSP. Many Member States believe that there are overriding common European foreign policy interests. Some Member States argue that the second pillar should be brought closer to the first pillar to improve coordination. German Foreign Minister Kinkel has argued that the IGC must do for the CFSP what the TEU did for EMU. Another German view is that if a fully functioning CFSP does not come into being, there may be a 'German Europe' rather than an 'European Germany'. There is currently no hegemon within the EU; if there is no EU, there would be one. By contrast, the UK questions whether more QMV in the second pillar would improve EU security and prevent other tragedies, such as Bosnia. It questions whether the CFSP might be a lowest common denominator, the result of continuous compromise between the Commission and the Council. Therefore the real question is not whether or not individual Member States want a CFSP but whether an effective one can be constructed.

One means of building a more effective CFSP would be a partial communitisation of the second pillar. This would provide: more consistency in all aspects of the EU's external policy; broader participation of EU institutions including the Commission or Council Secretariat playing a more active role in the field of analysis, planning and implementation of joint actions; and consolidating CFSP expenditures within the EU budget, giving the EP greater control over the entire spectrum of expenditure, while allowing for the possibility of recourse, in exceptional cases, to national contributions.

The CFSP could also be made more effective through the creation of an Analysis and Planning Unit, within the framework of the General Secretariat of the Council. Experts from Member States and the Commission would contribute to the formulation of common EU assessments and approaches to problems which today are subject to a diverse national approaches.

A further idea is the proposal by a 1994 expert group commissioned by Hans van den Broek to create a post of High Representative for CFSP, a 'Mr' or 'Mrs' CFSP, who would represent the EU in matters of foreign policy and project a stronger EU personality to the world. The President of the Council together with the Commission could take direct charge of CFSP affairs. However, it is feared that the powers of this new personality and that of the Council President would become confused. Furthermore, there is no consensus on how to appoint a Mr or Mrs CFSP. Would he/she be a former Prime Minister or national security adviser, with his/her own political weight? Would he/she be part of the Commission who would preside over a bureaucracy composed of MFA and Commission nominees? What would be the career structure?

Although it appears that the IGC is unlikely to change the CFSP fundamentally, the objectives of the CFSP should be better defined at the IGC. Such objectives should include: respect for human rights and democratic freedoms; a contribution of the EU to conflict prevention and stability, mainly in the CEECs, the Balkans and the Mediterranean Basin; protection of the EU's external frontiers, and the adoption of an EU solidarity and mutual assistance clause.

The unanimity rule is considered to be one of the main reasons for the CFSP's ineffectiveness. Nevertheless, consensus has not always prevented Europeans from taking vital decisions on security and defence matters in other fora, such as NATO and the WEU. In order to overcome the risk of deadlock in arriving at common policies, a number of options have been suggested:

general substitution of QMV for unanimity, with the exception of the use of military force. This option is supported by many Member States. However, many of those favouring QMV also argue that a fundamental or vital national interest may be invoked to prevent a common position or joint action;

introduction of 'constructive abstention'. Abstention would not stand in the way of unanimity. Although an abstaining Member State would not take part in the implementation of a joint action, it would still be required to demonstrate full political solidarity and to pay its share of the military operation;

introduction of an opt-out. This would exempt a Member State not only from actually taking part in the implementation of a joint action but also from displaying active and possibly financial solidarity.

The question arises whether these options do not risk leading to the exact opposite results of those intended, namely the EU, at worst, speaking with many voices or, at best, speaking with one voice, which the outside world knows does not have unanimous support within the EU itself.

There is little doubt that the implementation of the collective defence commitments embodied both in Article 5 of the Washington Treaty and Article V of the modified Brussels Treaty will, in practice, continue for the forseeable future to be secured within the NATO framework. Therefore the EU needs first and foremost to forge its own common security arrangements in order to deal with threats which, by their very nature, do not necessarily fall within NATO's scope. The Common European Security and Defence should be seen as complementary to the Atlantic Alliance and not as antithetical to it.

Today the threat is not of a large scale attack against a Member State but, rather, of local crises, and conflicts. The latter can be addressed through the missions set out by the WEU in the Petersberg Declaration, namely, humanitarian and rescue opera-tions, peace-keeping and tasks of combat forces in crisis management, including peace enforcement. The 'Petersberg Tasks' should be incorporated in the new EU Treaty, thus reflecting the changed nature of security in the new geo-political environment in which the EU has to operate. This option would also facilitate Member States of the EU which wish to contribute to European security by participating in the 'Petersberg Tasks', but without entering into collective defence commitments such as those defined in Article 5 of the Brussels and Washington Treaties. Neutral and non-aligned members of the EU will thus be able to involve themselves more actively in the EU's emerging security dimension.

On the one hand, WEU is part of the process of European integration and the EU's defence component, while on the other it is a military organisation, functionally closer to NATO, as its European pillar. The varying perceptions of Member States are often indicated by whether they put the emphasis on the first or second function. For some partners, the review of the CFSP should aim to establish a genuine European security and defence while for others "it should aim to reinforce NATO as the bedrock of European security while strengthening the overall contribution which European countries can make to global and regional security".

WEU Ministers in May 1996 "recalled their objective of making further progress toward defining and organising a European security architecture which meets the needs of a (stable) European continent". In its contribution to the IGC, the WEU proposed various options regarding its future. One option, a WEU-EU merger, would overcome the separation established at Maastricht, and create a single institutional defence identity. This would bring about greater coherence in European actions and a faster and more effective elaboration and implementation of decisions. Joint actions for crisis management and peace-keeping ('Petersberg Tasks') would be more easily undertaken. In the meantime, the EU should conclude a legally binding agreement whereby the WEU will undertake to carry out the EU's decisions and action, in particular the 'Petersberg Tasks'. The WEU will be in a position to carry out some 'Petersberg Tasks' by the end of

1996 now that the concept of military forces answerable to WEU (FAWEUS) has been defined and that NATO's Coordinated Joint Task Forces have been created.

New EU members would qualify for WEU membership. However, the question arises whether the WEU would be prepared to extend security guarantees of Article V to the newcomers, or whether the Brussels Treaty should be modified, leaving the CEECs outside. Membership in the WEU is closely linked with accession to NATO but some Member States argue that the latter is a prerequisite for the former.

Justice and Home Affairs

Co-operation in Justice and Home Affairs (JHA), or the third pillar, serves to further objectives of the EU such as creating a single market and achieving freedom of movement within the Community. The third pillar covers several areas: joint customs and police, external borders, extradition, terrorism, asylum, fraud, visas, money laundering, and the trafficking of nuclear substances and drugs. These matters remain almost entirely the responsibility of individual Member States. But growing economic interdependence, greater freedom of travel, and the breaching of the Iron Curtain, mean that Europe has become an area open to international organised crime, illegal immigrants and terrorists. Many Member States therefore believe that the fight against international crime must also be countered at the European level. Accordingly, Member States at Maastricht gave co-operation in JHA, which had previously been carried out exclusively on the basis of international law, a formal foundation under the EU's institutional umbrella.

There is widespread agreement that co-operation in the third pillar has been minimal and inefficient. Failed co-operation cannot be attributed to the provisions of the TEU, but rather to a lack of clear and unambiguous political will amongst Member States. This is primarily because the third pillar reaches the very heart of national sovereignty: decision-making by unanimity in the Council does not work.

There is agreement in principle between Member States on the fundamental desirability of improving European co-operation. However there are differences of opinion on how the necessary progress should be achieved. A few Member States believe that natural geographic boundaries and other factors suggest national and inter-governmental efforts are more appropriate. Many other Member States want a fundamental improvement by communitising items previously covered by inter-governmental co-operation. For example, visa and asylum policy, regulations governing the external borders, policies on immigration and freedom of movement within Community territory for third country nationals, the combating of drug addiction and of fraud, and co-operation in customs and civil cases should be communitised. One French view even argues that the IGC should abolish the third pillar and transfer it entirely to the first pillar in order to ensure that the EU becomes a society based on the rule of law. Another approach to improve co-operation envisages making better use of the existing regulations on co-operation provided for in the third pillar, but leaving the regulations themselves more or less unchanged.

The German Government believes that any clarifications to and improvements upon the TEU must go hand in hand with the formation of clear objectives and the building of political will amongst all Member States to make use of the third pillar instruments at their disposal. Specifically, better co-operation could be promoted by communitising all the policies relating to visas and asylum law. Germany believes every effort must be made to prevent the situation whereby different legal standards in individual Member States can be used in a calculated manner to enable a person to enter one Member State and obtain residence rights, and then use the right of freedom of movement within the Community to move on to the country which was his or her original destination. The present inadequate division of the areas of competence between the first and third pillars suggests that visa policies in the EU should be communitised. The objective of an open Community territory, within which freedom of movement is possible without internal border controls, can only be justified when there are uniform regulations and standards for crossing external EU borders. Progress here depends upon whether Spain and the UK resolve their dispute over Gibraltar.[3]

Other than visa and asylum policy, it is difficult to identify other areas suitable for communitisation. The same arguments which suggest that asylum policy should be harmonised can also be used to argue for the harmonisation of admission conditions for those refugees who do not fall within the scope of application of the Geneva Convention but to whom Member States may grant protection for humanitarian reasons.

In the case of mass refugee movements, Germany believes that communitising arrangements should not lead to one Member State being burdened unilaterally by the mass admission of refugees from a civil war and then having its hands tied on the question of repatriation by other Member States, which have assumed a much smaller part of the burden. Thus, in the German view, an important precondition for the communitising of the admission and repatriation of refugees in the case of mass refugee movements is the availability of an efficient system for burden sharing between Member States.

Given the increase in smuggling and illegal immigration, it is important that co-operation at the European level between police forces is strengthened. The path to more effective co-operation between European police forces began with the agreement to establish EUROPOL at the European Council in Luxembourg in 1991. However, improved co-operation remains elusive, even though the EUROPOL Convention, signed on 26 July 1995, represents a consensus at the EU level on how to combat international organised crime. The convention must still be ratified by Member States. A solution to the dispute over the competence of the European Court of Justice (ECJ) to make preliminary decisions must be found. Furthermore, a series of

---

[3] The EU's external borders remain undefined in the absence of a convention on external borders.

provisions on how to implement the convention and an adequate institutional framework must be developed if co-operation is to be improved. The EUROPOL convention itself provides instruments with which EUROPOL can be adapted for future tasks. Thus, for example, the areas of competence of EUROPOL can be extended gradually in accordance with Article 2 of the convention. The way is also open for the Council to include additional criminal areas by unanimous resolution. Thus intensification of the co-operation is already possible within existing rules. However, the option of communitisation should be kept open.

The IGC should create an even more flexible set of regulations which allows Member States to react independently to unknown future situations. Above all, Germany wants an article supplementary to Article K.9 of the TEU relating to all areas of the third pillar, thus creating a future option which would communitise EUROPOL in accordance with Article K.9. procedures. Preconditions would be an unanimous resolution of the Council and ratification in all the parliaments of signatory states. The urgent objective must be to implement legal provisions and to co-operate to the degree necessary. Ratification of the EUROPOL Convention by Member States would immediately bring about an effective joint instrument for exchanging and evaluating information centrally from many sources.

Institutional changes to improve co-operation must be discussed in the IGC. In particular, it is important to clarify the binding effect of the legal instruments stipulated in Article K.3 of the TEU. Germany has requested that there be a standard procedure to settle disputes relating to all legally binding instruments of Article K.3 within the competence of the European Court. Germany believes that it may also be expedient to increase the participatory rights of the EP in this and other third pillar areas. Concrete improvements on the basis of Article K.6 already exist. Germany also believes that the Commission should have the right of initiative in all third pillar matters. An active Commission could help overcome pressures from Member States and from the EU Presidency. However, Member States' right of initiative should remain untouched even if individual parts of the third pillar are communitised.

The Schengen Agreement

Another issue for the IGC is whether the Schengen Agreement, which lies outside the third pillar, should be included in a new EU Treaty. The Schengen system represents the only functional and effective means of police co-operation within the EU. On 26 March 1995, the Schengen Implementation Agreement came into force in Belgium, France, Germany, Luxembourg, the Netherlands, Portugal and Spain, thus contributing to real freedom of movement within Europe. However, France, citing the threat of terrorism, did not remove its border controls.

Since the Convention on the Application of the Schengen Agreement came into force, cross-border police co-operation has progressed rapidly although not all the possibilities provided under Articles 39 to 47 have been fully exploited. The Schengen database, which works within three minutes, has 10 million files with around 20 billion pieces of information. The network of bilateral agreements with the Schengen neighbouring states on operational services is growing. For example, Germany has already concluded agreements with Luxembourg, France and the Netherlands. These improvements are believed to have contributed to a tenfold increase in the number of arrests.

In addition to growing co-operation within the Schengen group, relationships with non-Schengen members is also growing. Scandinavian countries are seeking a link with the Schengen group. The three Nordic EU Member States, the only countries that can formally join the Schengen group in accordance with Article 140 of the Schengen Agreement, have insisted that a special arrangement be established for Iceland and Norway in order that the benefits of the northern passport union and the freedom of movement for passenger traffic are not abandonned. The Schengen states have the political will to bring in Iceland and Norway in some form of association. However, the only way to completely remove identity checks at common borders is within the framework of the Schengen system so that the compensatory and security instruments can be applied.

Intensification of the tracing and searching measures should also be achieved with cross-border co-operation in internal border areas. The final objective is for the Schengen Agreement to be incorporated into the EU. It is for this reason that Schengen should function unhindered and be retained as an impetus for EU development. However, if the Schengen were incorporated into the EU now, the integration process could be brought to a standstill, and the Schengen process would be slowed or hindered by an abstract debate. Similarly, it would be harmful if the effective fight against crime and illegal immigration was impaired by institutional disputes similar to that on the ECJ's jurisdiction over EUROPOL.

7   Parallel Issues

Member States decided not to discuss even more contentious issues such as EMU, competitiveness, employment, and reform of the CAP and Structural Funds at the IGC. The latter two issues will be discussed in 1999 when the EU budget is reviewed. In early 1998, Member States will decide which countries qualify to enter Stage Three of EMU. As developments in building EMU will influence the outcome of the IGC, and as some Member States want a chapter on competitiveness and employment in a new treaty, these two issues are examined here.

Economic and Monetary Union

EMU will have a more profound effect on the EU than the IGC. The balance of power in the EU will change. Those qualifying for Stage Three, the 'ins', will sit on the European System of Central Banks, and are likely to vote as a bloc in the Council on economic *as well as* fiscal issues (EMU thus necessitates a fiscal union). Some of the other Member States, the 'outs', are unlikely to qualify for Stage Three for a long time. As the TEU did not elaborate rules for those left behind in a second speed EMU, the role of the 'outs' in EU economic decision-making will be problematic.

Although they are likely to qualify for Stage Three, the UK and Denmark have not decided whether they wish to opt-in and join EMU. By contrast, many South European countries want to join, but are unlikely to qualify. Unlike northern Member States, there has been little debate in most South European Member States about EMU. This can be attributed largely to South European politicians not wanting to stimulate a debate on uncomfortable decisions, such as deep cuts in public expenditure, that EMU would oblige Southern European governments to make.

The TEU leaves room for political judgement in the interpretation of the EMU criteria. Many, including Germany, believe that the criteria must be adhered to, otherwise the stability of the Euro would be lost and EMU would become meaningless. For example, if Belgium is admitted to EMU with a high public debt ratio of 130 per cent of GDP, then Spain may ask for similar treatment. If Spain is admitted then Italy would demand admission to Stage Three as well. Yet for some in southern Europe, EMU could provide a convenient excuse for politicians to reduce high public debt levels, and join the European core.

Five possible scenarios for the future can be envisaged: EMU is postponed until every Member State qualifies for EMU; there is a multi-speed à la carte EMU in which Member States who meet the criteria decide whether or not they want to join EMU; EMU is not introduced properly, in part because the TEU's provisions are unclear; there is a sudden overnight entry by qualifying Member States in order to avoid massive currency speculation, or the entire EMU project is abandonned.

These scenarios are hotly contested. One Italian view is that Italy and Spain can and must qualify at the same time as others because a two-speed EMU would tear the EU apart. The 'ins' and 'outs' problem, especially in the context of an enlarged EU, can only be resolved if everyone is fully subject to the disciplines of being 'in'. However, most Northern countries believe EMU cannot wait for all Member States to qualify at the same time; EMU cannot be postponed for another 26 years. Stage Three of EMU will be launched on schedule in 1999 with many Northern Member States participating. EMU will therefore proceed at different speeds.

Competitiveness and Employment

Member State governments had to face some uncomfortable facts in mid-1993 when the Commission's White Paper portrayed a decline in EU competitiveness compared to that of the United States and Japan over twenty years, and a steady increase in unemployment from business cycle to business cycle. Member State Governments have taken different lines in attempting to account for the relative decline in EU competitiveness according to their political and ideological orientations.

The British government was quick to attribute the decline to high costs and inflexibility arising from protective social legislation prevalent elsewhere in the EU. It maintained that the British workforce is more flexible than those of other EU countries because hiring and firing is much easier and wages are not artificially boosted by minimum wages. It also argued that its deregulation policies have been more successful than those of other EU Member States in combating unemployment and stimulating growth. This is substantiated by the UK's success in attracting almost half of the EU's inward foreign direct investment from the Far East and the United States.

The British government's assertion that high labour costs and inflexibility arise from protective social legislation is at the heart of its continuing opposition to a common EU social policy. The Social Chapter, an annex to the TEU agreed by the then 12 Member States, empowered Member States except the UK to use EU institutions to introduce social policy in specified areas. The Social Chapter aims to provide a common and level playing field thoughout the EU which would extend QMV to a wider range of social issues, thus avoiding the normal requirement of unanimity in decision-making. However, the areas of social policy in which

QMV apply are limited: occupational health and safety; equal opportunity for men and women; working conditions; information and consultation of workers, and the integration of those excluded from the labour market. Other areas of social policy were introduced into the competence of the EU but require unanimity: social security and social protection; protection of workers where their employment contract is terminated; representation and collective defence of the interests of workers and employers, including co-determination; conditions of employment for third country nationals legally residing in EU territory, and financial contributions for promotion of employment and job creation. Specifically ruled out of EU competence by the TEU were pay, the right of association such as to form and join trade unions, the right to strike and the right to impose lock-outs.

The TEU protocol accorded to the social partners, unions and employers, a role in formulating policies in the areas specified in the Social Chapter. The purpose was to introduce flexibility and to extend application of the principle of subsidiarity. In practice this offers scope to trade union and employers' organisations to reach framework agreements to give effect to Commission proposals, providing an alternative to legislation proposed by the Commission to the Council of Ministers. This should have been a useful channel to build cooperation, but so far only one agreement on parental leave has been reached.

In practice, little use has been made of the opportunities opened up by the Social Chapter. A directive on information and consultation rights in multinational companies has been adopted. The directive does not apply to the UK but more than 30 UK companies have established machinery for informing and consulting their employees in line with the steps taken in other EU Member States. The British government tried to block the working time, the burden of proof in equal pay, and atypical work directives without success. Other legislation proposing to protect the pay and conditions of workers posted elsewhere in the EU and workers' rights on the transfer of ownership of an undertaking are being blocked.

However, the ECJ's principle of direct effects means that a Member State may be forced to pay damages for any harm caused to an individual as a consequence of a Member State's failure to give full effect to a relevant directive. For example, in 1995 the English Appeal Court ruled that the law in the UK relating to unfair dismissal and sexual equality is incompatible with EU law. This, and other cases, show that individuals may hold governments responsible for failing to guarantee their entitlements under EU law.

So foreign investors which choose to invest in the UK are unlikely to base investment decisions on differences between the UK and the rest of the EU in respect of social policy. In reality the Social Chapter has made very little difference to company costs. Companies locate in the UK for other reasons: use of the English language, the presence of a skilled work force, location, tax breaks and government subsidies.

In spite of the EU's apparent declining competitiveness, the entrenched Christian Democratic and Social Democratic traditions throughout most of the EU mean that complete abandonment of the European social model, the envy of many, is not an option. Higher wages and enhanced social rights are widely believed to have fostered a more committed and skilled workforce which is ready to embrace, and even initiate, innovation. Although the higher social costs associated with European social policies may have contributed to higher unemployment, especially in Southern Europe, they have contributed to overall social and industrial peace.

Advocates of the continental social model argue that is not possible to isolate the impact of deregulation, employment flexibility and the UK's opt-out from the Social Chapter, as factors contributing to the UK's recent economic success. Wages are not the only cost to companies: they are only important if all other factors, such as transport costs, and access to raw materials and the market, are equal. Far from encouraging flexibility, the move to low paid, insecure employment undermines the flexibility which stems from improvements in skills and training and adaptation to new technologies. Employers have little incentive to invest in developing people if the workforce is not stable. The fall in UK unemployment since the end of 1992 cannot be associated with any strong increase in employment using ILO definitions and the Labour Force Survey. Up to the end of 1994, the increase in the numbers in work was less than the fall in ILO defined employment. Many of the new jobs which have been created in the last ten years and described as full time are in reality precarious and insecure. The new jobs are sometimes the result of employers breaking up full time jobs and introducing poor quality, low pay, and part time jobs. Temporary employment is a large component of net employment growth in the last two years. Furthermore, the current economic performance of the UK cannot be compared with that of the continent because the UK's economic upswing usually precedes that of continental EU economies. Finally, with the changes in the pattern of world production, the UK's low wage strategy could leave it unable to compete in both high *and* low value added sectors. In industrial sectors where low wages is all that matters, no country can compete with emerging giants such as China and India!

8 What Will the IGC Achieve and When?

It is unlikely that any major EU Member State will call for the IGC process to be wound-up before the next British general election. The Conservative Government's thin majority means that the vocal Eurosceptic minority within the Conservative parliamentary party has a disproportionate influence on government policy. In actual fact, there is a majority in the UK Parliament in favour of futher European integration. Anti-European sentiment in the Conservative Party appears to be growing, especially amongst younger members, while any previous split within the opposition Labour party is diminishing as older Members of Parliament retire.

The political debate in the UK about the EU mirrors a split in British public opinion.[4] In the public debate on European issues, the popular tabloid newspapers have played a less than constructive role. The tabloids have become increasingly hostile towards Europe as the declining fishing industry and the beef crisis have brought to the surface renewed popular fears of a loss of sovereignty to Brussels. In order to increase circulation, the tabloids have cynically exploited instinctive fears of the unknown and the unfamiliar. For example, Britain's European neighbours are painted as either a threat to her well-being, or even as objects of ridicule. Even serious UK newspapers, such as *The Times* and *The Daily Telegraph* convey the same hostile and ill-informed sentiments, albeit in less crude terms. In so doing, tabloid editors succeed in appealing to the most basic instincts of 20 million readers, more than half of the UK's adult population.

Until shortly before the Turin Summit, it was fairly straightforward what the IGC would achieve and when it would be completed. The IGC would probably end within four months following the last possible date after the British General Election, between June and September 1997. Based on current opinion polls, the Labour party in the UK has a commanding lead in the opinion polls. An incoming Labour government would be more accommodating in the IGC than the current government. However, a final IGC package negotiated by a Labour government would probably not achieve a radically different result: there would be no grandiose redesign of the structures of Europe; there would be no historic turning point in the development of Europe, and not enough would have been done to enable enlargement, or the problems of a two or multi-speed EMU. In short, there would probably have to be yet another IGC in 1999.

Whilst this may still be the most likely outcome, the beef crisis and the UK's temporary policy of non-co-operation before the Turin Summit made another outcome possible. The UK's non-co-

---

[4] Sir Leon Brittan stated in *The Financial Times* of 16 May 1996 that many Britons simply 'lack confidence'.

operation policy is believed to make it less likely that other Member States will want to make concessions to the UK in the IGC. It is alleged that France and Germany agreed to a flexibility clause in the Turin communique partly, if not largely, out of exasperation with the UK's position. The flexibility clause has potentially changed the basis for a final IGC package, and it widens the range of possible outcomes from the IGC. It could mean more drastic, even dangerous, changes in the nature of Europe. It offers the possibility of *permanent* variable geometry, not just multi-speeds, and permanently different structures for full EU Member States. The espousal of permanent variable geometry with a flexibility clause would have certain attractions for many key Member States. It means the federalist states and the Commission would not be held back by one Member State. Yet it would also allow any government to opt-out permanently from policies decided by unanimity that it does not wish to adopt.

Variable geometry already exists to some extent with the opt-outs from the Social Chapter and EMU. If 13 Member States agree on incorporation of the Schengen agreement into a new treaty, the variable geometry of the EU would become even more entrenched. Advances on citizenship and the CFSP may also be refused by a number of EU governments. The UK government, therefore, may not be the only government that 'takes advantage' of the Turin flexibility clause.

The IGC could end up with a minimalist package which 'tidies up' the first pillar and keeps the other two pillars as they are. A more radical outcome, but in many ways a bad scenario, would be if the IGC institutionalises permanent variable geometry for the long term. In either scenario, the IGC is unlikely to have resolved the fundamental challenges of enlargement. Nor will the future defence structure of Europe have been resolved. The impact of a two-speed EMU, the issues of the budgetary position for Europe post-1999 and post-enlargement will not have been fully taken into account. Restoring confidence of the citizens in EU institutions will also still need to be addressed.

British Policy

The UK government currently maintains that the EU's three pillar structure is appropriate. The CFSP should be strengthened with the WEU having a closer relationship with the EU. However, the UK opposes the WEU being subordinated to, and then merged with, the EU. This could jeopardise NATO. It opposes a CFSP decided by QMV on the grounds that such a CFSP would not be common. The French idea of a 'Mr CFSP' is believed to be worth examining. The UK believes that co-operation in the third pillar has been more effective than is commonly alleged. A more efficient third pillar is possible within existing inter-governmental mechanisms. The UK is against extending the scope of majority voting but it does favour a reweighting of votes in the Council to reflect the size of population. The UK favours an increased role for national parliaments in European decision-making but it opposes giving more power to the EP. In order to better reflect the importance of larger Member States, there should be team Presidencies lasting one year. The UK wants to increase scrutiny of the ECJ's decisions and to ensure that EU legislation is more coherent. The UK would continue its opt-out of the Social Chapter and, for the time being, EMU.

EU Member States can expect a considerable change in the UK's tone if Labour is elected. The European policy of an incoming Labour government will be crucial in defining and concluding the final IGC package. An incoming Labour government might be more forthcoming in many areas, but there will still be some difficulties in reaching unanimous decisions.

Opting back into many parts of the TEU would cause Labour both electoral and, in some cases, internal difficulties. It is difficult for Labour to distance itself from government policy. Labour realises that it must express conditional support for the Conservative Government's European policies in order to win over the majority of British voters. Labour is therefore giving few hostages to fortune because it recognises that the pro-Tory press and the Conservatives are ready to 'savage' pro-European policies. As the IGC progresses, UK public opinion is likely to be increasingly wound up by the xenophobic UK press. By the time of the general election, it may be clear that the Conservatives would opt out of several areas where progress is being made. The challenge to Labour, therefore, is whether or not it should state unequivocally that it would reverse existing opt-outs. If it does, Labour risks being criticised for 'selling out' Britain, whereas the Tories would argue that they have 'defended' the national interest.

It would be unwise for the other 14 Member States to discount the possibility of obtaining a better deal from the Labour Party than from another Conservative government. The Labour approach to Europe, despite some continuity of a national interest and attitude, would probably be much more pro-active and pragmatic. A Labour government would negotiate constructively to help conclude a final Treaty. Labour would seek allies both bilaterally and through the network that the Party of European Socialists offers.

A Labour government would oppose variable different speeds and permanent exclusion. It would not introduce a complete end to voting by unanimity and there will be no full communitisation of the second and third pillars. Although Labour's position on the second and third pillars is not that different from that of the present British government, in the first pillar, Labour policy is considerably different. Labour would wish to sign up to the Social Protocol and bring it into the main part of the TEU. Labour would support moves for an employment chapter in the Treaty. Labour would wish to extend provisions on environment, and would be prepared to consider significant extensions of the citizenship provision, the incorporation or endorsement of the European Convention on Human Rights and measures against racism and xenophobia.

Labour will adopt a 'wait and see' policy regarding the single currency. Different views exist within Labour with some seeing the single currency as the harbinger of massive budget cuts. However, the majority of the Labour Party and the trade unions favour joining Stage Three of EMU from its inception. Nevertheless, Labour would prefer postponing a decision on the single currency for a year or two. Accordingly it will call for a referendum on the single currency.

On the issue of voting in the Council of Ministers, Labour would insist on greater transparency where the Council acts as a legislative body, and it would like to see a move towards reweighting votes in favour of the larger states, not so much in an EU of 15, but in an EU of 25 Member States. Labour would be prepared to see QMV extended to the areas of regional, industrial, environmental, and cultural policy, where unanimity still applies. QMV could also apply to various administrative areas and appointments. These areas would, however, have to exclude those relating to taxation and social security systems. The precise balance may depend on a deal between the extension of QMV and the reweighting of votes.

Labour would be substantially more positive than many current governments concerning the EP. Labour would want some simplification of the legislative process with co-decision extended to all legislation where QMV applies. Other procedures should be reduced to assent or consultation. Simplication of the co-decision procedure would allow national parliaments more time to play a greater role. Labour would wish to see a merger of the compulsory and non-compulsory elements of EU expenditure, thus giving the EP full control over the community budget. In so doing, reform of the CAP would be easier. The EP would also have more powers over appointments, particularly of individual Commissioners, rather than the Commission as a whole. An extraordinary majority, perhaps two thirds of MEPs, should be able to request the retirement of a specific Commissioner.

Labour would not seek to limit the role of the ECJ. Labour would support some of the reforms called for by the Conservative White Paper 'A Partnership of Nations' but it would also favour some others such as single terms for judges appointed to the ECJ, and a requirement for clearer written judgements.

Concerning the second pillar, Labour has a similar position to the Conservative government. Labour believes that decisions on defence should continue to be inter-governmental and that on key decisions, unanimity should continue to apply. Greater use could be made of the existing J.3.2 provisions allowing for consequential decisions to be taken by QMV, but Labour is not attracted by the proposals for 'constructive abstention' or unanimity minus one. Either a common foreign policy is common to all, or it is not. Labour does not favour developing an EU defence capability. In the parallel discussions on the future of the WEU, Labour favours a positive development of that organisation and possibly of dividing its responsibilities between the Petersburg crisis management tasks and Article 5 territorial requirements that the latter should be pursued within the aegis of NATO and a WEU developed as the European arm of NATO. The former could be still be part of the WEU, but a part which the neutral EU states could also support and which would need to act in conjunction with EU political requirements. However, Labour does not favour the incorporation of the WEU into the EU. In any case, the renegotiation of the WEU Treaty will probably not take place until after the IGC is completed.

Concerning the third pillar, Labour would again, but for different reasons, have a similar position to the Conservative government. Labour would oppose the communitisation of the pillar and it would oppose any dilution of unanimity voting. However, Labour favours some rationalisation of procedures, and it would favour more resources being used in the common fight against drugs, terrorism, and fraud. It also supports the establishment of an effective EUROPOL. Labour would, however, not favour the ECJ having a role within this inter-governmental area. Labour recognises that this area must be subject to detailed discussion because legislation has civil rights implications. Labour opposes any incorporation of the Schengen proposals into the first pillar, as well as the Monti proposals for free movement because their implementation would provoke xenophobic public reactions. Although generally the rights of third country nationals within the UK are better than those of third country citizen rights elsewhere in the EU, the UK has an entirely different system of security control, depending almost entirely on border controls, rather than internal security and identity cards, which UK citizens do not want to change.

9   Conclusions

1. There is a growing mood amongst Member States favouring a more flexible EU, possibly even a permanent variable geometry EU. Aware that unanimity will be difficult to achieve, the IGC is currently in a tactical phase characterised by Member States waiting to see how the political situation develops in the UK. Given that a UK general election will most likely take place around April 1997, the IGC will probably finish in mid-late 1997. Most substantive negotiations will therefore take place in the summer following the formation of the next British Government.

2. It is widely believed that a new treaty should have a flexibility clause. A more flexible, 'differentiated' EU can be characterised by 'Ten Commandments': all Member States should participate; a minimum number of Member States can participate in a 'core'; the single EU institutional framework is respected; the *acquis communautaire* is respected; flexibility should not distort EU activity; flexibility must be temporary; flexibility is used as a last resort; flexibility cannot be enshrined in any treaty change; decisions on flexibility should be made unanimously; and flexibility must be controlled by the ECJ or the Commission (in order to ensure uniform legislation and implementation). There is probably the most scope for flexibility in the third pillar. However, the 'Ten Commandments' have already been violated by the Danish opt-out of EMU and the British opt-out of the Social Chapter.

3. Only modest changes can be expected to the TEU. However, existing EU treaties may be sufficient to enact change. A final, *and minimalist*, IGC package is likely to include: strategies to keep EU integration moving forward with formal clauses for flexibility, variable geometry and multi-speeds (transitional phases and opt-outs); incorporating the Schengen agreement

within the TEU; extension of QMV in the Council to culture, research and development, indirect taxation and three environmental areas; lowering of voting theshholds in the Council; simplified and more transparent decision-making procedures; more co-decision for the EP with the Council; more rotation of the Council Presidency; a reduction in the number of Commissioners, and a partial 'communitarisation' of the second and third pillars.

4. The IGC will therefore not provide a quantum leap forward in European co-operation, largely because it is not addressing many contentious areas such as reform of the CAP and Structural Funds, competitiveness and employment, and EMU. Some, therefore, believe that the IGC should place more emphasis on substantive issues and less on the principle of flexibility.

5. As the IGC is likely to produce only modest results, another IGC in 1999 or 2001 may be required to prepare the EU fully for enlargement. Another IGC could further damage the credibility of the EU.

6. Any new treaty will need to be accepted by citizens of the EU. If the man in the street is persuaded about the benefits of EU, then political problems will fade away. Transparency is one way of helping to sell the EU to its citizens. Improving the transparency of EU decision-making does not require treaty changes because it can be achieved through more majority voting.

7. It is widely believed that QMV should be used for making most Council decisions with a limited number of well-defined exceptions such as the budget, constitutional change and tax where unanimity should be retained.

8. There is no need for an unproductive confrontation between large and small Member States in the IGC. Smaller Member States fear that larger states will use the IGC to increase their weighted vote in Council decision-making. However, EU decision making is not characterised by differences between large and small Member States, but by interests found equally among small and large states depending upon the issue. A final IGC deal is likely to

give more weighted voting to larger states, possibly in return for allowing smaller states to continue having one Commissioner.

9. EU legislative procedures should be simplified and reduced to improve transparency and democratic accountability. A more democratic voting threshhold in the Council would be 60 per cent, reflecting *both* a simple majority of Member States and a simple majority of the EU's population. The EP's power of co-decision should be extended to areas where the Council decides by QMV. Opinion is mixed as to whether this should become the main procedure for legislation.

10. National parliaments should be more involved in examining EU legislation. However, like the EP, they can only exercise influence over the Council and Commission if they are informed of proposed legislation in good time.

11. Although there is agreement between the Member States on the desirability of improving co-operation in the third pillar, there are fundamental differences of opinion on how progress should be brought about. Some argue that better use of existing regulations could be made. A number of Member States hope that visa and asylum policy, regulations governing external borders, immigration policy, freedom of movement within the EU for third country nationals, the combatting of drug addiction and of fraud, and co-operation in customs and civil cases can be 'communitised'. Others believe that such JHA issues should be simply moved from the third to the first pillar.

12. The EU must have an effective CFSP, especially for matters that are outside NATO's scope. However, it is unlikely that the CFSP will be changed considerably in the foreseeable future. One possible change is a partial 'communitarisation' of the second pillar providing more consistency in all aspects of the EU's external action, and the greater participation of EU institutions. For example, the Commission or Council Secretariat could play a more active role in analysing, planning and implementing joint actions; the inclusion of CFSP expenditure in the EU budget would give the EP a greater role in all aspects of the CFSP. The

'Petersberg' tasks, namely humanitarian and rescue operations, peace-keeping, and crisis management operations, should be incorporated in a new EU Treaty. Member States should also express a clear commitment to protect external borders and stipulate a clause of mutual assistance in case of external aggression. Discussions within the IGC on more QMV, 'constructive abstention' and opt-outs risk leading to results opposite to those intended: namely the EU, at worst, speaking with many voices and, at best, speaking with one voice, which is widely recognised as not being the unanimous view of EU Member States.

13. The bovine spongiform encephalopathy (BSE) crisis in the UK highlights the gap that can grow between the EU and its citizens. In order to avoid another such crisis being replicated elsewhere in the EU, national politicians should be more pro-active in fostering informed national debates about the EU.

14. For electoral reasons, the Labour Party in the UK is demonstrating conditional solidarity with the UK's government's EU policy, for fear that its more pro-European policies would be criticised for 'selling out' Britain. Thus, on the face of it, an incoming Labour Government would only change the atmosphere of the UK's relations with other Member States. However, on the bulk of EU issues, a future Labour government would probably be more positive than the present government and would be prepared to compromise in the IGC. Labour would end the UK's Social Chapter and EMU opt-outs, and would possibly join the first phase of EMU in 1999. Labour would extend QMV to some areas and it would extend co-decision to the EP to areas where the Council decides by QMV. There would be some changes in the second pillar but UK policy on the third pillar would remain unchanged.

Lists of Participants

469:

ARCHIBALD, Liliana: Wilton Park Academic Concil, London
BARTORELLI, Paolo: Ministry of Foreign Affairs, Rome

BEILFUSS, Burkart: Vertretung der Freien und Hausestadt, Bonn
BERNATOWICZ, Grazyna Maria: Ministry of Foreign Affairs, Warsaw
BERNET, Luzi: "Zurichsee Zeitung", Stafa
BIERING, Peter: Ministry of Foreign Affairs, Copenhagen
BOND, Martyn: United Kingdom Office of the European Parliament, London
BRATT, Christian: Swedish Employers' Confederation, Stockholm
BURGER, Cornelis: Ministry of Foreign Affairs, The Hague
CHATZIVASSILIOU, Despina: Council of Europe, Strasbourg
COLLECOTT, Peter: British Embassy, Bonn
D'ANDRIA, Antonio: Ministry of Foreign Affairs, Rome
ENGEL, Hans: Ministry of the Interior, Dusseldorf
EVANS, Nigel: European Commission, Brussels
FELLNER, Irmgard Maria: Ministry of Foreign Affairs, Bonn
FLYNN, Sean: "The Irish Times", Dublin
FURGLER, Dominik: Federal Ministry of Foreign Affairs, Bern
GARRONE, Pierre: Council of Europe, Strasbourg
GRUBER, Andrea: Ministry of Defence, Vienna
GUIMOND, Pierre: Department of Foreign Affairs and International Trade, Ottawa
GUNDERSEN, Fridtjof: Member of Parliament, Oslo
HARASIMOWICZ, Andrzej: Council of Ministers' Office, Warsaw
HAVLIK, Jiri: Embassy of the Czech Republic, London
HENNIG-BURNS, Petra: Federal Ministry of the Interior, Bonn
HENSELER, Peter: Federal Ministry of Finance, Vienna
HOPKINSON, Nicholas: Wilton Park, Steyning
HOUMANN, Alan: H M Treasury, London
JENNINGS, Colin: Wilton Park, Steyning
JERVELL, Sverre: Ministry of Foreign Affairs, Oslo
KELERHALS, Andreas: Europa Institute, Zürich
KISCHEL, Dieter: Federal Ministry of Finance, Bonn
KOSTER, Timo: Ministry of Foreign Affairs, The Hague
LACHNIT, Hans-Wilhelm: Federal Ministry of Defence, Vienna
LEONARDI, Robert: The European Institute, London School of Economics and Political Science, London
LEVEAUX, Bertrand: Ministry of Foreign Affairs, Paris
LEVER, Paul: Foreign and Commonwealth Office, Paris

LIPKA, Grazyna: Council of Ministers' Office, Warsaw
LUDLOW, Peter: Centre for European Policy Studies, Brussels
MARCUSE, Elie: NATO, Brussels
MARTIN, Geoffrey: European Commission Representation to the
  United Kingdom, London
MELAN, Andreas: Federal Ministry for Foreign Affairs, Vienna
MIJALKOVIC, Djorde: Embassy of the Federal Republic of
  Yugoslavia, London
MILNER, Colin: Australian Mission to the European Union,
  Brussels
OLBERG, Petter: Ministry of Foreign Affairs, Oslo
PAUL, Jan-Peter: VR Group Ltd, Finnish Railways, Helsinki
PULLINEN, Matti Johannes: Ministry for Foreign Affairs,
  Helsinski
SAUDARGAS, Algirdas: Christian Democratic Party, Vilnius
SCHELTER, Kurt: Federal Ministry of the Interior, Bonn
SCHMUCK, Vertretung des Landes Rhineland-Pfalz, Bonn
SCHOCHLI, Hansueli: "Der Bund", Bern
SMITS, Aloysius: Royal Netherlands Airforce, The Hague
STATHATOS, Stephane: Hellenic Foundation for European and
  Foreign Policy (ELIAMEP), Athens
STEINBACH-van der VEEN, Brita: Deutsche Bundesbank -
  Fachhochschule, Hachenburg
STUBB, Alexander: Ministry for Foreign Affairs, Helsinki
TANNER, Teemu: Ministry for Foreign Affairs, Helsinki
TOFT, Ole: Ministry of Foreign Affairs, Copenhagen
VERANNEMAN, Jean-Michel: Embassy of Belgium, London
WASLANDER, Jacob: Ministry of Foreign Affairs, The Hague
WEY, Marc: Federal Ministry of Foreign Affairs, Bern
WHITTY, Larry: Labour Party, London
WIESNER, Peter: Confederation of German Industry, Cologne
WILCOCK, Ian: Australian High Commission, London
ZURAWSKI vel GRAJEWSKI, Przemyslaw: Council of Ministers'
  Office, Warsaw

453:

AIZSTRAUTS, Igors: Foreign Affairs Bureau, Latvian Parliament,
  Riga
AMATI, Aldo: Italian Embassy, London

BAIER, Klaus: Austrian Federal Chamber of Labour, Vienna

BELIUS, Thomas: Ministry of Foreign Affairs, Stockholm

BOND, Martyn: United Kingdom Office of the European Parliament, London

CARVALHO, Josefina: Ministry of Foreign Affairs, London

CHRISTOFFERSEN, Poul Skytte: Permanent Representation of Denmark to the European Union, Brussels

COWELL, Andrew: Foreign and Commonwealth Office, London

CROWE, Virginia: Wilton Park, Steyning

CZACHOR, Zbigniew: Council of Ministers' Office, Warsaw

DE BONT, Emiel: Ministry of Foreign Affairs, The Hague

DENTON, Geoffrey: European Cultural Foundation; Federal Trust, London

DOWNING, John: "Irish Independent", Brussels

DUNCAN-SMITH, Iain: Conservative Member of Parliament, London

EHALA, Katrin: Foreign Affairs Committee, Parliament, Tallinn

FASEL, Alexandre: Federal Department of Foreign Affairs, Berne

FEDARAU, Andrey: International Relations Department, Supreme Council, Minsk

FORSTERLING, Wolfram: State Chancery of North Rhine Westphalia, Dusseldorf

FROMENT-MEURICE, Francois: Conseiller d'Etat, Paris

GALPIN, Albert: Department of Foreign Affairs and International Trade, Ottawa

HALD-MADSEN, Jens: Liberal Member, Danish Parliament, Copenhagen

HALL HALL, Alexandra: European Secretariat, Cabinet Office, London

HARASIMOWICZ, Andrzej: Council of Ministers' Office, Warsaw

HAVLIK, Jiri: Embassy of the Czech Republic, London

HELLSTROM, Mats: Minister for Foreign Trade, European Union Affairs and Nordic Cooperation, Stockholm

HIRDMAN-SANDBERG, Tonika: Ministry of Foreign Affairs, Stockholm

HOFFMANN, Henning: Ministry for Federal and European Affairs, Berlin

HOPKINSON, Nicholas: Wilton Park, Steyning

JAY, Michael: Foreign and Commonwealth Office, London

JESIEN, Leszek: Council of Ministers' Office, London
JOHANNESSON, Stefan: Ministry of Foreign Affairs, Reykjavik
JUSZCZYK, Jurek: Australian Embassy, The Hague
KAUFMANN-BÜHLER, Werner: Federal Ministry of Foreign Affairs, Bonn
KEHOE, Stephen: British Aerospace, Brussels
KETTERER, Juan Antonio: InterMoney S A, Madrid
KLINGENBECK, Dieter: Federal Ministry of Finance, Bonn
KOSKIMIES, Tapio: Defence Forces, Helsinki
KRAEVSKI, Hristo Tonchev: Center for Information and Public Relations, National Assembly, Sofia
LAUFER, Thomas: Cabinet of the President, German Federal Parliament, Bonn
LIPKA, Grazyna: Council of Ministers' Office, Warsaw
MANGIN, Florence: Ministry of Foreign Affairs, Paris
MARITZ, Daniel: Federal Department of Foreign Affairs, Bern
MEINHART, Maria-Theresia: Federal Ministry of Defence, Vienna
MILNER, Colin: Australia Embassy, Brussels
NEIFER-DICHMANN, Elisabeth: Federal Ministry of Social and Labour Affairs, Bonn
NOGA, Vologymyr: Commission on Budget Issues, Ukrainian Parliament, Kiev
NOORMAN, Ernst: Ministry of Foreign Affairs, The Hague
O'LEARY, Eoin: Prime Minister's Office, Dublin
OPPENHEIMER, Walter: "El Pais", Brussels
ORSZAGH, Veronika: Office for Foreign Relations, National Assembly, Budapest
PITROVA, Lenka: Parliamentary Institute, Chamber of Deputies, Prague
PLASCHE, Wolfgang: Federal Ministry of Defence, Vienna
POPESCU, Daniel: International Department, Parliament, Bucharest
PORIAS, Hannes: Ministry of Foreign Affairs, Vienna
PYDYCHOVA, Veronika: Foreign Affairs Department, National Council, Bratislava
QUIN, Joyce: Labour Member of Parliament, London
RASMUSSEN, Annegrethe: "Weekendavisen", Copenhagen
ROMMEL, Krzysztof: Interparliamentary Relations Bureau, Sejm, Warsaw

SEDELMEIER, Ulrich: European Institute, University of Sussex, Brighton
SHAW, Alan: Foreign and Commonwealth Office, London
SMYTH, Patrick: "Irish Times", Brussels
SPANGGARD, Ib: Minish of Agriculture and Fisheries, Copenhagen
STANKEVICIUS, Rimantas: National Security Committee, Parliament, Vilnius
STENWALL, Lena: Ministry for Foreign Affairs, Stockholm
STURMER, Michael: Stiftung Wissenschaft und Politik, Ebenhausen
THÜRER, Daniel: Europa Institute, Zürich
TULBURE, Alexei: Interparliamentary Relations Department, Parliament, Kishinev
VAAGEN, Lars: Ministry of Foreign Affairs, Oslo
van der ZWAN, Gerard: Ministry of Foreign Affairs, The Hague
van LOENEN, Piet: Ministry of Economic Affairs, The Hague
WALSH, Michael: International Department, Trades Union Congress, London
WIEBEL, Markus: Federal Court Judge, Karlsruhe
WILCOCK, Ian: Australian High Commission, London
WILLIAMS, Keith: SEED Programme, North Atlantic Assembly, Brussels
YENNIMATAS, John: Ministry of Foreign Affairs, Athens
ZBINDEN, Martin: Institut de Hautes en Administration Publique (IDHEAP), Chavannes

Printed in the United Kingdom for the Stationery Office by Hobbs the Printers
Dd303345 02/97 C3 G3397